# Learn C Programming
## through Nursery Rhymes and Fairy Tales

By Shari Eskenas

Illustrated by Ana Quintero Villafraz

SUNDAE
ELECTRONICS

Published by Sundae Electronics LLC
https://www.sundaelectronics.com

First edition 2023

ISBN 978-1-7359079-9-4 (Hardcover)
ISBN 979-8-9881835-0-1 (Paperback)
ISBN 979-8-9881835-3-2 (eBook)

# Table of Contents

Dear Apprentice,

I'm so glad you've arrived at C Castle! A magical experience awaits you- you'll see computer code transformed into classic nursery rhymes and fairy tales!

Once upon a time in a faraway land, there was an enchanted computer deep in the woods. The computer told nursery rhymes and fairy tales using **code**, which is a set of instructions written for a computer to perform tasks, such as printing text to the screen or playing a video.

A **program** is a collection of code that can be run by a computer. The enchanted computer told the nursery rhymes and fairy tales using programs written in the **C programming language**. Every programming language has its own set of rules for how the code is written, which is called the **syntax**. Different programming languages are written with different syntax and designed for different uses.

People from the nearby village occasionally wandered into the forest and listened to the enchanted computer's stories. Over the years, the C programs stored on the computer were written down and recorded in a book. You will now be presented with these C programs. **Your journey has just begun!** There are instructions at the end of this book for running the enchanted programs on **YOUR** computer!

Warm Regards,
S.E.

# Jack Be Nimble

Jack be nimble,
Jack be quick,
Jack jump over the candlestick

```c
#include <stdio.h>

int main(void)
{
    printf("Jack be nimble, Jack be quick, Jack jump over the candlestick");

    return 0;
}
```

Lines of code can be separated with empty lines to make the code easier to read. A **keyword** is a reserved word that has a special meaning in C, such as int and return that are described below.

A **statement** is a complete program **instruction** that is run (executed) by a computer to perform an action. A program's statements are executed from top to bottom. The first statement in this program is printf("Jack be nimble, Jack be quick, Jack jump over the candlestick").

main() is a **function**. A function is a block of code (within curly braces) that contains instructions to perform a specific task. Every C program needs a main() function, where the program begins running. It is considered good practice to indent the code within a code block, which makes it easier to read.

printf() is a function in the **C standard library** that **outputs** text to the computer screen. A **library** is a collection of predefined functions, data, and other resources that can be used in your programs. The C standard library is provided with your **C compiler**, which converts your C code into machine instructions for the computer and links your program with the standard library.

A function's code block is run (executed) when the function is called with its name followed by parentheses. The printf() function prints the **string** passed to it within the parentheses to the standard output device (typically a computer screen). A string is a sequence of characters—letters, numbers, symbols, or spaces—that is enclosed within double (") quotation marks when written in code. "Jack be nimble, Jack be quick, Jack jump over the candlestick" is passed to the printf() function as a string within double quotes. When the program is executed, the printf() function prints Jack be nimble, Jack be quick, Jack jump over the candlestick to the screen, without the double quotes.

stdio.h is a **header file** that contains information needed for the C standard library's **input** and **output** functions to work. This header file is needed to use the printf() function. It is included in the program with #include.

return 0 returns a value of 0 to the system running the program, which is typically used as a signal that the program successfully finished. The int before main() indicates the return value is an **integer** (a whole number that doesn't have a decimal point). The void indicates that the main() function does not receive any data.

# Row, Row, Row Your Boat

Row, row, row your boat
Gently down the stream
Merrily merrily, merrily, merrily
Life is but a dream

```c
// Row Your Boat

#include <stdio.h>

int main(void)
{
    printf("Row, row, row your boat\n");
    printf("Gently down the stream\n");
    printf("Merrily merrily, merrily, merrily\n");
    printf("Life is but a dream");

    return 0;
}
```

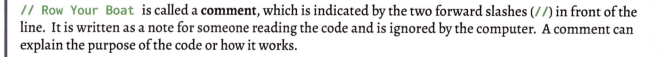

`// Row Your Boat` is called a **comment**, which is indicated by the two forward slashes (`//`) in front of the line. It is written as a note for someone reading the code and is ignored by the computer. A comment can explain the purpose of the code or how it works.

`\n` is a **newline character** that ends the line so that the next `printf()` will start printing at the beginning of the next line.

When the program is executed, the four `printf()` functions print the following text on the screen:

```
Row, row, row your boat
Gently down the stream
Merrily merrily, merrily, merrily
Life is but a dream
```

# Star Light, Star Bright

Star light, star bright,
First star *I* see tonight;
*I* wish *I* may, *I* wish *I* might,
Have the wish *I* wish tonight.

```c
// Make a wish on a star

#include <stdio.h>

int main(void)
{
    int star_order = 1;

    printf("Star light, star bright,\n");
    printf("Star number %d that I see tonight;\n", star_order);
    printf("I wish I may, I wish I might,\n");
    printf("Have the wish I wish tonight.");

    return 0;
}
```

`star_order` is called a **variable**. A variable stores a value in the computer's memory and the programmer gives it a name. The variable can be given any name—`star_order` was chosen because it's a meaningful name. Before variables are used, they must be declared with a data type such as `int` for storing an integer. A variable's data type determines the type of data it can hold and how it can be used. For example, an integer can be added to another integer, but an integer can't be added to a string. Variables can be assigned a starting value (initialized) when they are declared. In this program, the variable `star_order` is declared as an `int` and initialized to `1`.

You assign a value to a variable with an equal sign (=), which is called an **assignment operator**. The value on the right side of the equal sign is assigned to the variable on the left side of the equal sign. **Operators** are special symbols that perform operations on values or variables. In this program, the integer `1` is assigned to the `star_order` variable.

`%d` is an integer **format specifier**. The format specifier consists of a percent sign `%` followed by a character that indicates the data type of the data to be displayed. In this program, `%d` is replaced by the value of `star_order` when `printf()` prints the text.

Variable names in C are conventionally written in lowercase letters and an underscore (_) separates words in the name because variable names cannot contain blank spaces. They can contain letters, numbers, and underscores. A variable name cannot start with a number.

The four `printf()` functions print these lines:
```
Star light, star bright,
Star number 1 that I see tonight;
I wish I may, I wish I might,
Have the wish I wish tonight.
```

# Rain, Rain, Go Away

Rain, rain, go away
Come again another day
Little Johnny wants to play.

```c
#include <stdio.h>

#define RAIN 1
#define NO_RAIN 0

int main(void)
{
    int weather = 1;

    if (weather == RAIN)
    {
        printf("Rain, rain, go away\n");
        printf("Come again another day\n");
        printf("Little Johnny wants to play.");
    }

    return 0;
}
```

#define allows a constant value to be represented by a name in the code called a **macro**. In this program, RAIN is a macro defined as the value 1 and the macro NO_RAIN is defined as the value 0. RAIN is replaced by 1 in main(). #define is called a **preprocessor directive** because the macro name is replaced by its value in every place it appears in the program before it is processed.

There is no semicolon at the end of a #define line. By defining a constant value with a meaningful name, the code is easier to read and you can change the constant's value in a single place. It's common to use uppercase names for macros to easily distinguish them from variables.

An if statement is a **conditional statement** that tests if a condition is true or false. An **expression** is a piece of code that evaluates to a single value. The expression within parentheses after if is the condition that is tested for being true or false. If the if statement's condition is true, its code block within curly braces {} is executed.

In the if statement's condition (conditional expression), weather == RAIN, the double equal sign (==) is called an **equality operator**. This is a type of comparison (relational) operator, which compares the relation between two values. The equality operator tests if the value on the left side of the operator is equal to the value on the right side of the operator. Since weather is a variable that stores the value 1 and RAIN is replaced by 1, the expression is true, so the if statement's condition is true and its code block is executed.

The printf() functions print:
Rain, rain, go away
Come again another day
Little Johnny wants to play.

# Jack and Jill

Jack and Jill went up the hill
To fetch a pail of water.
Jack fell down and broke his crown,
And Jill came tumbling after.

```c
#include <stdio.h>

#define UP 1
#define DOWN 0
#define TRUE 1
#define FALSE 0

int main(void)
{
    int jack_direction = UP;
    int jill_direction = UP;
    int jack_fall = FALSE;

    if (jack_direction == UP && jill_direction == UP)
    {
        printf("Jack and Jill went up the hill to fetch a pail of water.\n");
        jack_fall = TRUE;
    }

    if (jack_fall)
    {
        printf("Jack fell down and broke his crown,\n");
        printf("And Jill came tumbling after.");
    }
    else
    {
        printf("Mission accomplished.");
    }

    return 0;
}
```

In the first `if` condition, the **&&** operator is called the **logical AND operator**. It tests if the expression on the left of it is true AND the expression on the right of it is true. If both expressions are true, the overall condition evaluates to true. Conversely, if either expression is false or both expressions are false, the condition evaluates to false.

In this case, since `jack_direction == UP` is true and `jill_direction == UP` is also true, the `if` condition is true. Therefore, the `if` statement's code block is executed, and `jack_fall` is assigned the value `TRUE`.

An `if…else` statement allows one of two code blocks to be executed based on whether the condition is true or false. Any expression that evaluates to a non-zero value is considered true. Since `jack_fall` now has a value of `1`, the condition in the second `if` statement evaluates to true and the `if` code block is executed. Conversely, if the condition were not true, the `else` code block would be executed instead.

# Humpty Dumpty

Humpty Dumpty sat on a wall,
Humpty Dumpty had a great fall.
All the king's horses and all the king's men
Couldn't put Humpty together again.

```c
#include <stdio.h>

#define TRUE 1
#define FALSE 0

int main(void)
{
    int humpty_dumpty_together = TRUE, humpty_on_wall = TRUE, accident = FALSE;

    if (humpty_on_wall)
    {
        printf("Humpty Dumpty sat on a wall,\n");
        accident = TRUE;
    }

    if (accident)
    {
        printf("Humpty Dumpty had a great fall.\n");
        humpty_dumpty_together = FALSE;
    }

    if (!humpty_dumpty_together)
    {
        printf("All the king's horses and all the king's men\n");
        printf("Couldn't put Humpty together again.");
    }

    return 0;
}
```

Multiple variables can be declared on the same line if they are of the same data type. The variables humpty_dumpty_together, humpty_on_wall, and accident are all integers declared on one line by being separated by commas with int at the start of the line.

Since humpty_on_wall is initialized to FALSE, the first if statement is executed, which assigns TRUE to accident. This causes the second if statement to be executed, which assigns FALSE to humpty_dumpty_together.

The **NOT operator** is represented by the exclamation mark (!) symbol. When it's placed in front of an expression, it reverses the logical value of the expression. It changes true to false, and false to true. Therefore, the third if statement's condition evaluates to true since humpty_dumpty_together is false, which is inverted by the NOT operator to make the condition become true.

# Peter Piper

Peter Piper picked a peck of pickled peppers.
If Peter Piper picked a peck of pickled peppers,
Where's the peck of pickled peppers Peter Piper picked?

```c
#include <stdio.h>

#define PICKLED_PEPPERS 0
#define CHOCOLATES 1
#define FRUIT_CANDIES 2
#define GUMMY_BEARS 3

int main(void)
{
    int item_picked = PICKLED_PEPPERS;

    if (item_picked == CHOCOLATES)
    {
        printf("Peter Piper picked chocolates");
    }
    else if (item_picked == PICKLED_PEPPERS)
    {
        printf("Peter Piper picked a peck of pickled peppers\n");
        printf("If Peter Piper picked a peck of pickled peppers,\n");
        printf("Where's the peck of pickled peppers Peter Piper picked?");
    }
    else if (item_picked == FRUIT_CANDIES)
    {
        printf("Peter Piper picked fruit candies");
    }
    else if (item_picked == GUMMY_BEARS)
    {
        printf("Peter Piper picked gummy bears");
    }
    else
    {
        printf("Did Peter Piper pick anything?");
    }

    return 0;
}
```

An `if...else if...else` statement allows multiple conditions to be tested in sequence. Only the code block of the first true condition is executed. In this program, the first `else if` block is executed since `item_picked` was assigned the value of `PICKLED_PEPPERS`.

# One, Two, Buckle My Shoe

One, two, buckle my shoe
Three, four, knock at the door
Five, six, pick up sticks
Seven, eight, lay them straight
Nine, ten, a big fat hen.

```c
#include <stdio.h>

int numbers[10] = {1, 2, 3, 4, 5, 6, 7, 8, 9, 10};

int main(void)
{
    printf("%d, %d, buckle my shoe\n", numbers[0], numbers[1]);
    printf("%d, %d, knock at the door\n", numbers[2], numbers[3]);
    printf("%d, %d, pick up sticks\n", numbers[4], numbers[5]);
    printf("%d, %d, lay them straight\n", numbers[6], numbers[7]);
    printf("%d, %d, a big fat hen.\n", numbers[8], numbers[9]);

    return 0;
}
```

An **array** is a collection of variables called **elements** that have the same data type. The elements are stored in a block of memory in sequential order. An array is declared with the data type of its elements followed by the array name and number of array elements in brackets `[]`.

When an array is declared, you can initialize it by assigning it a list of comma-separated values enclosed in curly braces `{}`. In this program, `numbers` is an array that has `10` elements that are initialized with the integer values `1` through `10`. The array size could have been left out of the declaration (`numbers[]`), since the array size is automatically determined from the number of values in the initialization list.

An array element is accessed with its **index**, which is an integer value that represents its position in the array. The first element in an array starts at an index of `0`, so `numbers[0]` is the first array element, which has a value of `1`. The last array element is `numbers[9]`, which has a value of `10`.

The `printf()` functions print:
```
1, 2, buckle my shoe
3, 4, knock at the door
5, 6, pick up sticks
7, 8, lay them straight
9, 10, a big fat hen.
```

# Hickory Dickory Dock

Hickory, dickory, dock.
The mouse ran up the clock.
The clock struck one,
The mouse ran down,
Hickory, dickory, dock.

```c
#include <stdio.h>
#include <string.h>

int main(void)
{
    int clock_hour = 1;
    char mouse_run_direction[10] = "up";
    char first[] = "Hickory";
    char middle[] = "dickory";
    char last[] = "dock";

    printf("%s, %s, %s\n", first, middle, last);
    printf("The mouse ran %s the clock.\n", mouse_run_direction);
    printf("The clock struck %d,\n", clock_hour);
    strcpy(mouse_run_direction, "down");
    printf("The mouse ran %s,\n", mouse_run_direction);
    printf("%s, %s, %s\n", first, middle, last);

    return 0;
}
```

The **char** data type is used to represent a character such as a letter or number. A **string** is an array of characters that represent text such as words or sentences. mouse_run_direction is declared as a character array of size 10, which means it can hold up to ten characters. The **null character** \0 is automatically added as the last element of a string to indicate its end. Since it is initialized with the string up, the characters u, p, and \0 are stored in the first three elements of the array.

When declaring a character array that is initialized with a string, it's not necessary to specify the array's size. However, the size of the array is determined by the length of the string, which means there won't be enough space for additional characters if a longer string is assigned to the array later. mouse_run_direction is declared with an array size of 10, which allows it to accommodate the longer string down that is assigned to it later. The size of each array first, middle, and last is determined by the size of the string it is initialized to. For example, last has a size of 5 because dock has four characters and the null character is automatically added at the end.

%s is a **string format specifier** that printf() replaces with the actual string value passed to it. string.h is a header file in the C standard library that contains functions for performing string operations. strcpy() is a function declared in string.h that is used to copy a string from one location into another. It is used in this program to copy the string down into mouse_run_direction. The printf() functions print the following:

```
Hickory, dickory, dock
The mouse ran up the clock.
The clock struck 1,
The mouse ran down,
Hickory, dickory, dock
```

# Hey Diddle Diddle

Hey diddle, diddle!
The cat and the fiddle,
The cow jumped over the moon;
The little dog laughed
To see such sport,
And the dish ran away with the spoon

```c
#include <stdio.h>

#define CAT 0
#define FIDDLE 1
#define SPOON 2
#define MOON 3
#define COW 4
#define LITTLE_DOG 5

int main(void)
{
    int thing_chosen;
    char name[] = "diddle";

    printf("Hey %s, %s!\n", name, name);
    printf("The cat and the fiddle\n");
    printf("The cow jumped over the moon\n");
    printf("The little dog laughed\nTo see such sport,\n");
    printf("And the dish ran away with ");

    thing_chosen = SPOON;

    switch (thing_chosen)
    {
        case 0:
            printf("the cat");
            break;
        case 1:
            printf("the fiddle");
            break;
        case 2:
            printf("the spoon");
            break;
        case 3:
            printf("the moon");
            break;
        case 4:
            printf("the cow");
            break;
        case 5:
            printf("the little dog");
            break;
        default:
            printf("nothing");
            break;
    }

    return 0;
}
```

A switch statement is an alternative to using a long if…else if…else statement to test if an integer value or a character value is equal to a value in a list. The expression in parentheses after switch is tested for a match in a list of case values. If there is a matched value in the list, one or more statements associated with the matched value are executed. When a break statement is reached, the switch statement is exited. The default label is optional, and its code block will be executed if there is no matched value in the case list.

Since thing_chosen was assigned the value of SPOON, which is 2, the case 2 code block is executed, which prints the spoon. Since there was no newline in the previous printf(), And the dish ran away with the spoon is printed as the last sentence.

# One Potato, Two Potatoes

One potato, two potatoes,
Three potatoes, four!
Five potatoes, six potatoes,
Seven potatoes, more!

```c
#include <stdio.h>

int main(void)
{
    int potato_count = 0;

    for (int i = 0; i < 7; i++)
    {
        potato_count = potato_count + 1;

        if (potato_count == 1)
        {
            printf("One potato\n");
        }
        else if (potato_count == 4)
        {
            printf("four!\n");
        }
        else
        {
            printf("%d potatoes\n", potato_count);
        }
    }

    printf("more!");

    return 0;
}
```

A for loop repeats a code block (within curly braces {}) for a specified number of times. In this program, the loop repeats (iterates) 7 times to count 7 potatoes. The loop's header, for(int i = 0; i < 7; i++), declares i as an integer and initializes it to 0. Although the for loop variable can be any valid name, the variable i (representing "index") is commonly used in C programming. Next, this process is followed:

Step 1. The condition i < 7 is tested for being true or false.
Step 2. If the condition is true, the for loop's code block is executed. If it's false, the code block is not executed and the program continues by jumping to the line of code after the for loop.
Step 3. After the code block executes, i++ increases i by 1 with the increment operator ++.

Steps 1 through 3 are repeated until the condition i < 7 is false (when i = 7), at which point the program exits the for loop.

In the for loop, the statement potatoes = potatoes + 1 assigns the value of potatoes + 1 to potatoes, which increases the potatoes value by 1 using the **addition operator** (+). Since the loop repeats 7 times and potato_count was initialized to 0, the value of potato_count is 7 when the for loop is exited.

The if…else if..else statement within the for loop's code block causes a particular printf() statement to execute based on the potato_count value.

# Little Bo-Peep

Little Bo-Peep has lost her sheep,
and doesn't know where to find them;
leave them alone, and they'll come home,
bringing their tails behind them.

```c
#include <stdio.h>

#define AT_HOME 1
#define NOT_AT_HOME 0

int main(void)
{
    int sheep_at_home[5] = {0};
    int sheep_count = 5;

    for (int i = 0; i < 5; i++)
    {
        if (sheep_at_home[i] == NOT_AT_HOME)
        {
            printf("Sheep number %d is not at home\n", i + 1);
            sheep_count--;
        }
    }

    if (sheep_count == 0)
    {
        printf("\nLittle Bo-Peep has lost her sheep\n");
        printf("and doesn't know where to find them\n");
        printf("leave them alone, and they'll come home\n");
        printf("bringing their tails behind them.");
    }

    return 0;
}
```

An array's elements can be initialized to 0 by assigning 0 within curly braces {0} to the array when it is declared.

In this program, the for loop iterates (loops through) each array element by using the loop variable i as an index to access each array element. The first array element is sheep_at_home[0], since the first element of an array always starts at an index of 0. Since every array element was initialized to 0, the if statement within the for loop is true for every element. Since the index i starts at 0, the sheep number value in printf() is i + 1, so Sheep number 1 is not at home is printed in the first iteration of the for loop.

The sheep_count value is decreased by 1 (decremented) using the **decrement operator** that is represented by two minus signs --. Since the for loop iterates 5 times and sheep_count is decremented in every loop iteration, sheep_count has a value of 0 when the for loop is exited. Therefore, the next if statement outside of the for loop is executed and the nursery rhyme is printed.

# Twinkle, Twinkle, Little Star

Twinkle, twinkle, little star,
How *I* wonder what you are!
Up above the world so high,
Like a diamond in the sky.
Twinkle, twinkle, little star,
How *I* wonder what you are!

```c
#include <stdio.h>

int main(void)
{
    char star_material[30];
    int star_num;
    char star_size[] = {'l', 'i', 't', 't', 'l', 'e', '\0'};

    printf("Twinkle, twinkle, %s star, how I wonder what you are!\n", star_size);
    printf("Up above the world so high,\nLike a diamond in the sky.\n");
    printf("Twinkle, twinkle, %s star,\n", star_size);
    printf("How I wonder what you are!\n");

    printf("What is the star made out of?\n");
    fgets(star_material, 30, stdin);
    printf("Enter a number for the star: \n");
    scanf("%d", &star_num);
    printf("Star number %d is made out of %s\n", star_num, star_material);

    return 0;
}
```

The `star_material` array was given a length of `30` to provide enough space for any possible strings that may be assigned to it. The `star_size` array is initialized to the string `little` with comma-separated character values. A character is represented in code by enclosing it within single (') quotation marks. When you initialize a string this way, the null character `\0` must be included at the end since it's not automatically added and is needed to mark the end of the string.

`fgets()` is a function that reads a line of text from a file or "standard input" (usually the keyboard) and stores it into a character array (string). The input is provided to `fgets()` through `stdin`, which is the "standard input" stream. The maximum number of characters to be read and stored into `star_material` is specified as `30` in `fgets()`. The `fgets()` function stores the input into `star_material` with a newline character `\n` at the end (since you pressed Enter on your keyboard after typing the text) and automatically adds a null character `\0` to the end of the string.

The `scanf()` function is used to read user input of different data types. In this program, `scanf()` reads an integer input into `star_num` using the `%d` format specifier. The ampersand `&` operator is used in `&star_num` because it is required before a variable in `scanf()` that is not a string. It is important to note that `scanf()` can only read and store the first word of a string input until it encounters a whitespace character (such as a space, tab, or newline). Therefore, `fgets()` should be used to read text input that may contain spaces.

# I'm a Little Teapot

*I'm a little teapot,*
*Short and stout,*
*Here is my handle*
*Here is my spout*
*When I get all steamed up,*
*Hear me shout,*
*Tip me over and pour me out!*

```c
#include <stdio.h>
#include <string.h>

struct Teapot
{
    char size[10];
    char height[10];
    int steam_level;
};

int main(void)
{
    struct Teapot t1; //Declare structure variable
    strcpy(t1.size, "stout");
    strcpy(t1.height, "short");
    t1.steam_level = 8;

    printf("I'm a little teapot\n");
    printf("%s and %s\n", t1.height, t1.size);
    printf("Here is my handle\nHere is my spout\n");
    printf("When I get all steamed up, hear me shout\n");

    if (t1.steam_level > 5)
    {
        printf("Tip me over and pour me out!");
    }

    return 0;
}
```

A **structure** is a custom data type that groups variables together, which allows you to create a collection of related information. A structure's data fields are called **members**, and they can be of different data types. A structure is defined using the keyword struct with the structure's members declared within curly braces {}. The structure's name is given after the struct keyword.

In this program, the structure is named Teapot. The Teapot structure contains two char array members and one int member. t1 is declared as a Teapot structure variable.

The dot operator (.) is used to access members of a structure. The steam_level member of t1 is assigned a value of 8. Since the dot operator cannot be used to assign values to multiple array elements at once, char arrays cannot be assigned strings with the dot operator. The string copy function strcpy() is used to assign strings to the size and height members. The string stout is assigned to the size member of t1 and the string short is assigned to the height member of t1. The printf() functions print the following:

```
I'm a little teapot
short and stout
Here is my handle
Here is my spout
When I get all steamed up, hear me shout
Tip me over and pour me out!
```

# The Muffin Man

Do you know the muffin man?
The muffin man, the muffin man.
Do you know the muffin man
Who lives in Drury Lane?

```c
#include <stdio.h>
#include <string.h>

typedef struct
{
  char name[15];
  char home_street_name[20];
} Person_t;

int main(void)
{
  char response;
  Person_t person_1;

  strcpy(person_1.name, "the muffin man");
  strcpy(person_1.home_street_name, "Drury Lane");

  printf("Do you know %s?\n", person_1.name);
  printf("%s, %s. Do you know %s?\n", person_1.name, person_1.name, person_1.name);
  printf("Who lives in %s?\n", person_1.home_street_name);
  printf("Enter Y or N: ");
  scanf("%c", &response);

  if (response == 'Y')
  {
      printf("So you DO know the muffin man!");
  }
  else
  {
      printf("I don't know him either");
  }

  return 0;
}
```

The keyword typedef allows you to create a new name (alias) for an existing data type. In this program, typedef is used in the struct definition to create a new struct data type called Person_t. When you use typedef to create a new name for a struct data type, you can declare variables of that type without using the struct keyword. person_1 is declared with the Person_t data type created using typedef. The first four print() functions print:

Do you know the muffin man?
the muffin man, the muffin man. Do you know the muffin man?
Who lives in Drury Lane?
Enter Y or N:

The scanf() function reads the single character input entered by the user with the %c character format specifier and stores the result in response. The if statement tests if response has the character value Y, in which case So you DO know the muffin man! is printed. Otherwise, I don't know him either is printed.

# Here We Go Round the Mulberry Bush

**1** Here we go round the mulberry bush,
The mulberry bush,
The mulberry bush.
Here we go round the mulberry bush
On a cold and frosty morning.

**2** This is the way we brush our teeth,
Brush our teeth,
Brush our teeth.
This is the way we brush our teeth
On a cold and frosty morning.

**3** This is the way we wash our face,
Wash our face,
Wash our face.
This is the way we wash our face
On a cold and frosty morning.

**4** This is the way we comb our hair,
Comb our hair,
Comb our hair.
This is the way we comb our hair
On a cold and frosty morning.

**5** This is the way we put on our clothes,
Put on our clothes,
Put on our clothes.
This is the way we put on our clothes
On a cold and frosty morning.

**6** Here we go round the mulberry bush,
The mulberry bush,
The mulberry bush.
Here we go round the mulberry bush
On a cold and frosty morning.

```c
#include <stdio.h>

//Function definitions
void mulberry_bush(void)
{
    printf("Here we go round the mulberry bush,\n");
    printf("The mulberry bush,\n");
    printf("The mulberry bush.\n");
    printf("Here we go round the mulberry bush\n");
    printf("On a cold and frosty morning.\n\n");
}

void how_to(char perform_action[])
{
    printf("This is the way we %s\n", perform_action);
    printf("%s\n", perform_action);
    printf("%s\n", perform_action);
    printf("This is the way we %s\n", perform_action);
    printf("On a cold and frosty morning.\n\n");
}
```

**Continued...**

There's a lot of repetitive text in this nursery rhyme! This situation is best handled with **user-defined functions**. A user-defined function is a block of code (within curly braces {}) that you create to perform a specific task. It allows you to reuse code without re-writing the code multiple times and makes the code more organized.

The first line of the **function definition** is called the function header (also called the function signature). The function name is followed by parentheses that can contain one or more **parameters** (also called **formal parameters**), which are variables that store information passed into the function. In this program, the `how_to()` function has a single parameter `perform_action[]` that is a character array. Since the function `mulberry_bush()` has no parameters, `void` is written in its parentheses.

A function can also return a value, whose data type is given before the function name. Since the two functions in this program don't return a value, `void` is written before each function name.

```c
        //Function prototypes
        void mulberry_bush(void);
        void how_to(char perform_action[]);

        int main(void)
        {
            //Function calls
            mulberry_bush();
            how_to("wash our face");
            how_to("brush our teeth");
            how_to("comb our hair");
            how_to("put on our clothes");
            mulberry_bush();

            return 0;
        }
```

You use a **function call** to execute (run) a function's code. The function call consists of the function's name followed by parentheses that contain values to be passed into any parameters it has. A value that is passed into a function's parameter is called an **argument**.

A function needs to be defined or declared before it is called. A **function prototype** is a function declaration that allows you to call a function defined after main(). The function prototypes are typically written above main(). The two function definitions on the previous page can be added to the program before or after the main() function.

In the first how_to() function call, "wash our face" is the argument that is passed into the perform_action parameter of the how_to() function. The perform_action value can then be used within the how_to() function. The how_to() function then prints:
This is the way we wash our face
wash our face
wash our face
This is the way we wash our face
On a cold and frosty morning.

When a function is called, the program transfers control to the function. After the function executes, the program resumes from where it left off after the function call. The next function call how_to("brush our teeth") is then executed. The six function calls in this program print the six verses of the nursery rhyme.

mulberry_bush() is a function call that doesn't have any arguments since the function doesn't have any parameters. It is used to print verses one and six of the nursery rhyme.

As you can see, a function allows a block of code to be re-used without typing it multiple times. As a result, this program is much shorter than the nursery rhyme it prints to the screen! Functions also make a program more organized and readable by breaking the program down into separate blocks of code.

# This Little Piggy

This little piggy went to market,
This little piggy stayed home,
This little piggy had roast beef,
This little piggy had none.
This little piggy went...
Wee, wee, wee,
all the way home!

```c
#include <stdio.h>

void piggy_activity(int piggy_number); //Function prototype

int main(void)
{
  for (int i = 1; i < 6; i++)
  {
      piggy_activity(i); //Function call
  }

  return 0;
}

void piggy_activity(int piggy_number) //Function definition
{
    printf("This little piggy ");
    switch (piggy_number)
    {
        case 1:
            printf("went to market\n");
            break;
        case 2:
            printf("stayed home\n");
            break;
        case 3:
            printf("had roast beef\n");
            break;
        case 4:
            printf("had none\n");
            break;
        case 5:
            printf("went wee, wee, wee, all the way home!\n");
            break;
        default:
            printf("doesn't exist\n");
    }
}
```

In the for loop, the piggy_activity() function is called with the current value of the loop variable i as the argument passed into the piggy_number parameter. This results in the program calling piggy_activity() five times, each time with a different argument from 1 to 5. In the first iteration of the for loop, the function call is piggy_activity(1), since the loop variable i starts at 1. In the last iteration of the for loop, the function call is piggy_activity(5). In the piggy_activity() function, a switch statement determines the printed output based on the value of piggy_number.

When the first function call is executed, This little piggy went to market is printed. When the last function call is executed, This little piggy went wee, wee, wee, all the way home! is printed. If the piggy_number value does not match a case value, This little piggy doesn't exist would be printed. This does not happen in the program since the function is called with arguments from 1 through 5.

# Goldilocks and the Three Bears

Once upon a time, there was a girl named Goldilocks who liked to play in the woods. One day as she was chasing butterflies in the forest, she arrived at a small house. Goldilocks knocked on the door, but no one was home. She smelled delicious food, so went inside. There were three bowls of porridge on the table. She tasted the large bowl of porridge, and it was too hot. She tasted the medium-sized bowl of porridge, and it was too cold. She tasted the small bowl of porridge, and it was just right, so she ate the whole bowl!

```c
#include <stdio.h>

enum {FALSE, TRUE};

enum size_e {SMALL = 2, MEDIUM, LARGE};

//Function prototypes
void porridge_test(enum size_e porridge_size);
void chair_test(enum size_e chair_size, int person_weight);
void bed_test(enum size_e bed_size);

void porridge_test(enum size_e porridge_size)
{
    if (porridge_size == LARGE)
    {
        printf("The large porridge is too hot\n");
    }
    else if (porridge_size == MEDIUM)
    {
        printf("The medium-sized porridge is too cold\n");
    }
    else if (porridge_size == SMALL)
    {
        printf("The small porridge is just right! I'll eat it.\n");
    }
}
```

**Continued...**

An **enum** is a data type defined using the enum keyword that assigns constant integer values to names. By default, the first name is assigned the value 0 and each subsequent name is assigned a value one greater than the previous name. In this program, FALSE has a value of 0 and the next named value TRUE has a value of 1. Enum names are typically capitalized to indicate they hold constant values.

There are two enums defined in this program because it's good practice to use enums to group related information together. An enum can be given a name like the enum named size_e in this program. By giving an enum a name, you can create a variable of that type. The porridge_test() parameter porridge_size is of the type enum size_e, which means porridge_size can only accept a value defined in the size_e enum.

Named values in an enum can be assigned any integer value, but if not specified, the default is to increment the previous value by 1. In this program, SMALL is assigned a value of 2, so MEDIUM is assigned 3 and LARGE is assigned 4.

Goldilocks looked for a place to sit and found three chairs. She sat in the large chair and it was too hard. She sat in the medium-sized chair and it was too soft. She sat in the small chair and it was just right. However, she exceeded the chair's weight limit of 50 pounds (as shown on the label) and the chair suddenly broke into pieces!

```c
void chair_test(enum size_e chair_size, int person_weight)
{
    if (chair_size == LARGE)
    {
        printf("The large chair is too hard\n");
    }
    else if (chair_size == MEDIUM)
    {
        printf("The medium-sized chair is too soft\n");
    }
    else if (chair_size == SMALL)
    {
        printf("The small chair is just right!\n");

        if (person_weight > 50)
        {
            printf("Oh no, it just broke into pieces!\n");
        }
    }
}
```

**Continued...**

A function can have multiple parameters, which are separated by commas. When the function is called, arguments must be separated by commas in the same order as the parameters in the function definition. The chair_test() function has the parameters chair_size and person_weight.

The chair_test() function contains if...else if...else if statements that test the value of chair_size to determine which message to print. If the value of chair_size is SMALL, the function prints The small chair is just right! and then checks the value of person_weight using another if statement nested inside the else if statement. It uses the **greater than operator** (>) to test if person_weight is greater than 50, in which case it prints Oh no, it just broke into pieces!

Goldilocks was looking for a place to rest and found three beds. She climbed into the large bed and it was too hard. She climbed into the medium-sized bed and it was too soft. She climbed into the small bed, and it was just right, so she fell asleep. The three bears who lived in the house returned from their walk and found Goldilocks asleep in the small bed. They woke her up and she ran out the door!

```c
void bed_test(enum size_e bed_size)
{
    if (bed_size == LARGE)
    {
        printf("The large bed is too hard\n");
    }
    else if (bed_size == MEDIUM)
    {
        printf("The medium-sized bed is too soft\n");
    }
    else if (bed_size == SMALL)
    {
        printf("The small bed is just right! I'll take a nap.\n");
    }
}

int main(void)
{
    int bears_home = FALSE;

    if (!bears_home)
    {
        printf("I'll go into the house because no one is home\n");
    }

    porridge_test(LARGE);
    porridge_test(MEDIUM);
    porridge_test(SMALL);

    int weight = 60;
    chair_test(LARGE, weight);
    chair_test(MEDIUM, weight);
    chair_test(SMALL, weight);

    bed_test(LARGE);
    bed_test(MEDIUM);
    bed_test(SMALL);
    printf("Run! The bears are home!\n");

    return 0;
}
```

The variable `bears_home` is assigned the enum value of `FALSE`, which is `0`. The NOT operator (!) inverts the value of `bears_home`, making the `if` condition true and printing the message `I'll go into the house because no one is home`.

The enum values of `LARGE`, `MEDIUM`, and `SMALL` are used as arguments in the function calls for `porridge_test()`, `chair_test()`, and `bed_test()`. Since `chair_test()` has two parameters, two arguments are included in the `chair_test()` function calls. The argument `weight`, which has a value of `60`, is passed into the `person_weight` parameter of `chair_test()`. Since this value is greater than `50`, the nested `if` statement in `chair_test()` is executed and `Oh no, it just broke into pieces!` is printed.

# The Three Little Pigs

Once upon a time, three little pigs lived with their mother. One day, they left home and set out to build their own houses. The youngest pig built a house made of straw in one day. The middle pig built a house made of sticks in three days. The oldest pig built a house made of bricks in seven days.

```c
#include <stdio.h>

#define GONE  0
enum {HOUSE_1 = 1, HOUSE_2, HOUSE_3};

void wolf_action(int* house_number); //function prototype

int main(void)
{
    int youngest_pig_house = HOUSE_1, middle_pig_house = HOUSE_2, oldest_pig_house = HOUSE_3;

    int* house_ptr = &youngest_pig_house;
    printf("\nThe youngest pig built house #%d in one day ", *house_ptr);
    printf("at address %p", house_ptr);

    house_ptr = &middle_pig_house;
    printf("\nThe middle pig built house #%d in three days ", *house_ptr);
    printf("at address %p", house_ptr);

    house_ptr = &oldest_pig_house;
    printf("\nThe oldest pig built house #%d in seven days ", *house_ptr);
    printf("at address %p", house_ptr);
```

**Continued...**

A **pointer** is a special variable that stores the **memory address** of another variable or value. While a normal variable holds a value that is stored at a memory address (a location in the computer's memory), a pointer "points" to this location by storing the memory address. A pointer is declared with the type of data it will point to, which is followed by an asterisk (*) and the name of the pointer variable. In this program, `house_ptr` is the name of a pointer that points to an `int` variable.

The **address operator** (&) is used in front of a variable to get its memory address. When `house_ptr` is declared, it is assigned the address of `youngest_pig_house`. The **dereference operator** asterisk (*) is used in front of a pointer name to access the data stored at the memory address it holds. The value stored at the address held by `house_ptr` is given by `*house_ptr`. Since `youngest_pig_house` has a value of 1, `*house_ptr` has a value of 1.

The first two `printf()` statements print `The youngest pig built house #1 in one day at address 0x7ffe2df5b1c4`. The `%p` format specifier is used to print the address, which will be specific to your computer's memory, so you may see a different value. `house_ptr` is re-assigned the address of `middle_pig_house`, and then re-assigned the address of `oldest_pig_house`. The remaining `printf()` statements print `The middle pig built house #2 in three days at address 0x7ffe2df5b1c8` and `The oldest pig built house #3 in seven days at address 0x7ffe2df5b1cc`. The `0x` in front of an address indicates that the address is in hexadecimal format, which is a way to represent numbers using a base of 16 (as opposed to decimal numbers, which use a base of 10).

Just as the little pigs were enjoying their new houses, The Big Bad Wolf arrived. He went to the house made of straw and shouted "Let me in little pig, or I'll huff and I'll puff and I'll blow your house down!" The wolf blew down the house made of straw. He went to the house made of sticks and shouted, "Let me in little pig, or I'll huff and I'll puff and I'll blow your house down!" The wolf blew down the house made of sticks.

```c
/* Call wolf_action() with the address of each pig's house variable and display a
   message if a house variable is set to GONE (0) after the function call */

wolf_action(&youngest_pig_house);
if (youngest_pig_house == GONE)
{
    printf("The youngest pig's house is gone!\n");
}

wolf_action(&middle_pig_house);
if (middle_pig_house == GONE)
{
    printf("The middle pig's house is gone!\n");
}

wolf_action(&oldest_pig_house);
if (oldest_pig_house == GONE)
{
    printf("The oldest pig's house is gone!\n");
}

return 0;
}
```

**Continued...**

When variables are passed as arguments into function parameters, they are **passed by value**. This means that a **copy** of the variable's value is passed into the function parameter, leaving the original variable's value unaffected. Although the function can change the value passed into it, this change doesn't impact the original variable. Instead, the new value can be returned to the function call line.

However, if a function parameter is a pointer, the address of a variable can be passed into it. This approach is called **pass by reference**. It allows the function to modify the variable's value directly, as it now has access to the original variable's memory location.

The wolf_action() function (defined on the next page) has the potential to change the value of the variable whose address is passed into it. Therefore, after the address of youngest_pig_house is passed into wolf_action(), the variable youngest_pig_house is checked to see if it has a value of GONE (0). The other variables whose addresses are passed into wolf_action() are also tested for having a value of GONE (0).

A multi-line comment allows you to write a comment that spans as many lines as you want. As demonstrated in the code above, it starts with a forward slash and an asterisk /* and ends with an asterisk and a forward slash */.

He went to the brick house and shouted, "Let me in little pig, or I'll huff and I'll puff and I'll blow your house down!" He tried to blow down the brick house, but it was too sturdy! The Big Bad Wolf went down the chimney of the brick house and fell right into a pot of boiling soup. He ran out of the house and never came back again. The three little pigs lived happily ever after.

```c
void wolf_action(int* house_number)
{
    printf("\nLet me in little pig, ");
    printf("or I'll huff and I'll puff and I'll blow your house down!\n");

    if (*house_number == 1)
    {
        printf("The wolf blew down the straw house!\n");
        *house_number = GONE;
    }
    else if (*house_number == 2)
    {
        printf("The wolf blew down the wood house!\n");
        *house_number = GONE;
    }
    else if (*house_number == 3)
    {
        printf("The wolf can't blow down the brick house!\n");
        printf("He went down the chimney and fell into a pot of boiling soup!");
    }
}
```

The `wolf_action()` function's parameter, `house_number`, is a pointer to an integer. Note that the asterisk that declares a variable to be a pointer can be placed anywhere between the data type and pointer name, so the parameter declaration could also be written as

`int * house_number` or `int *house_number`

The value stored in the address held by `house_number` is accessed by `*house_number` (using the dereference operator `*`). If `*house_number` has a value of `1`, the first `if` statement re-assigns it a value of `GONE` (`0`). This has the effect of changing the value of the variable whose address is passed into this function. If `*house_number` has a value of `2`, the first `else..if` statement re-assigns it a value of `GONE` (`0`). If `*house_number` has a value of `3`, its value is not modified.

Pointers are useful because they provide a way to access and manipulate memory directly. When used as function parameters, they enable the function to modify the actual data stored in memory, not just a copy of it.

# Jack and the Beanstalk

Once upon a time, a boy named Jack lived in a cottage with his mother. One day, she told him to go to the town and trade their cow for money. In the town, Jack was convinced by a strange man to trade his cow for magic beans. When he got back home, his mother was angry and threw the magic beans out the window. The next morning, Jack saw a huge beanstalk growing outside! He decided to climb it.

```c
#include <stdio.h>

enum {MAGIC_BEANS, GIANT_BEANSTALK, COW, MONEY};

int throw_into_yard(int item)
{
    if (item == MAGIC_BEANS)
    {
        printf("Why did you throw the magic beans out the window?\n");
        return GIANT_BEANSTALK;
    }
    return item;
}

int trade(int item)
{
    if (item == COW)
    {
        printf("I'll trade my cow for magic beans\n");
        return MAGIC_BEANS;
    }
    return MONEY;
}

void climb_beanstalk(int visit_num)
{
    switch (visit_num)
    {
        case 1:
            printf("I climbed the beanstalk and took back a bag of gold coins\n");
            break;
        case 2:
            printf("I climbed the beanstalk and took back a hen that lays golden eggs\n");
            break;
        case 3:
            printf("I climbed the beanstalk and took back a magical harp\n");
            printf("Oh no, the giant is chasing after me!\n");
            printf("I cut down the beanstalk. Now we can live happily ever after");
            break;
        default:
            printf("Invalid visit number. The beanstalk is gone!");
    }
}
```

**Continued...**

Functions can return a single value with the return value's data type specified in front of the function name. In this program, each function `trade()` and `throw_into_yard()` returns an `int` value to its function calling line. In `throw_into_yard()`, if `item` has a value of 0 (MAGIC_BEANS), `return GIANT_BEANSTALK` causes the function to exit with a return value of 1 (GIANT_BEANSTALK). Otherwise, the integer value of `item` is returned from the function. Similarly, in `trade()`, if `item` has a value of 2 (COW), the function exits with a return value of 0 (MAGIC_BEANS). Otherwise, the function returns with a value of 3 (MONEY).

Jack climbed up the beanstalk to a castle at the top, where a giant was sleeping. Jack took a bag of gold coins and climbed down the beanstalk before the giant woke up. Jack climbed the beanstalk again and took back a hen that laid golden eggs. After Jack climbed to the castle for the third time, he took a magical harp. The giant heard the harp play as Jack was leaving and he chased him down the beanstalk. Jack rushed down fast enough to cut the beanstalk before the giant could catch him. Jack and his mother lived happily ever after.

```c
//Function prototypes
int trade(int item);
int throw_into_yard(int item);
void climb_beanstalk(int visit_num);

int main(void)
{
    int in_yard;
    int received_item = trade(COW);

    if (received_item != MONEY)
    {
        in_yard = throw_into_yard(received_item);
    }

    if (in_yard == GIANT_BEANSTALK)
    {
        printf("A giant beanstalk just grew outside!\n");
        climb_beanstalk(1);
        climb_beanstalk(2);
        climb_beanstalk(3);
    }

    return 0;
}
```

The trade() function is called with an argument of 2 (COW) and the returned value of 0 (MAGIC_BEANS) is stored in received_item. Since the value of received_item is not equal to 3 (MONEY), the first if statement is evaluated as true. The throw_into_yard() function is then called with received_item as the argument. The throw_into_yard() function returns a value of 1 (GIANT_BEANSTALK) that is stored in in_yard.

Since in_yard holds a value of 1 (GIANT_BEANSTALK), the second if statement is evaluated as true and the climb_beanstalk() function is called three times. In the first call, an argument of 1 is passed into the function, which is used in the switch() statement to print I climbed the beanstalk and took back a bag of gold coins. In the second function call, the argument of 2 results in the printing of I climbed the beanstalk and took back a hen that lays golden eggs. In the third function call, the argument of 3 results in the following lines being printed:
I climbed the beanstalk and took back a magical harp
Oh no, the giant is chasing after me!
I cut down the beanstalk. Now we can live happily ever after

# Little Red Riding Hood

Once upon a time, there was a girl known as Little Red Riding Hood. One day, her mother asked her to bring a basket of food (cupcakes, cookies, and donuts) to her grandmother because she wasn't feeling well. As Little Red Riding Hood was walking through the forest to her grandmother's house, a wolf asked her where she was going. Little Red Riding Hood told the wolf she was going to granny's house.

```c
#include <stdio.h>

typedef struct
{
    int ears;
    int eyes;
    int hands;
    int teeth;
} Features_t;

enum {SMALL, MEDIUM, BIG};

const char HUNTER = 'H';
const char GRANNY = 'G';


#define IS_FEATURE_BIG(feature) (feature == BIG)

//Function prototypes
int wolf_test(Features_t features);
char scare_wolf(char person);
```

**Continued...**

In previous programs, a #define macro was used to substitute a symbolic name for a value. However, a macro can also be used to define an expression, which is a combination of code that evaluates to a single value.

In this program, we've defined a macro IS_FEATURE_BIG(feature) as a substitute for the expression (feature == BIG). When we use IS_FEATURE_BIG(feature), the value or variable we provide as its parameter feature is substituted for feature in the expression feature == BIG. This approach enhances the code's readability because IS_FEATURE_BIG instantly conveys the intent of the check.

In the wolf_test() function prototype, the features parameter is a Features_t structure.

A variable can be declared with the const modifier to indicate that its value is constant and won't change during the program's execution. You cannot re-assign the value of a const variable once it is set. The const variables HUNTER and GRANNY are capitalized to indicate they hold constant values. HUNTER is assigned the character H and GRANNY is assigned the character G.

Once she arrived at the house, she thought her grandmother looked peculiar. She exclaimed, "My, what big ears you have!", "My, what big eyes you have!", "My, what big hands you have!", and "My, what big teeth you have!".

```c
int wolf_test(Features_t features)
{
    int features_big = IS_FEATURE_BIG(features.ears) &&
                       IS_FEATURE_BIG(features.eyes) &&
                       IS_FEATURE_BIG(features.hands) &&
                       IS_FEATURE_BIG(features.teeth);

    if (features_big)
    {
        printf("My, what big ears you have! My, what big eyes you have!\n");
        printf("My, what big hands you have! My, what big teeth you have!\n");
        return 1;
    }
    else
    {
        return 0;
    }
}

char scare_wolf(char person)
{
    if (person == HUNTER)
    {
        printf("I'm a hunter and I'll scare the wolf with my axe!\n");
        return GRANNY;
    }
    else
    {
        return 0;
    }
}
```

**Continued...**

At the beginning of the `wolf_test()` function, the logical AND operator (&&) is used to check if all four expressions are true. An expression that is true evaluates to a value of 1. Each expression uses the `IS_FEATURE_BIG(feature)` macro to test if a `features` member is equal to BIG. For example, `IS_FEATURE_BIG(features.ears)` is substituted with (`features.ears == BIG`), which tests if the value of `features.ears` is equal to BIG. If each expression is true (1), then the overall result of the operation is true (1). In this case, the `if` statement evaluates to be true and a value of 1 is returned from the function. If any expression is false (0), then the overall result is false (0) and the function returns 0.

In the `scare_wolf()` function, if the `person` variable holds the character H, the `if` statement is evaluated as true because the constant variable HUNTER stores the character H. In this case, the function returns GRANNY, which holds the character G. If the value of `person` is not H, the `else` statement is executed, and the function returns 0.

Little Red Riding Hood then realized a wolf was in granny's clothing and she screamed. A hunter heard her and ran into the house. He scared off the wolf with his axe and recovered Little Red Riding Hood's grandmother.

```c
int main(void)
{
    Features_t features_seen;
    features_seen.ears = BIG;
    features_seen.eyes = BIG;
    features_seen.hands = BIG;
    features_seen.teeth = BIG;

    printf("Hi Granny!\n");
    int big_result = wolf_test(features_seen);

    if (big_result)
    {
        printf("Oh no, it's a wolf!\n");
    }
    else
    {
        printf("I brought you cupcakes, cookies, and donuts\n");
    }

    char person_rescued = scare_wolf(HUNTER);

    if (person_rescued == GRANNY)
    {
        printf("Granny and Little Red Riding Hood are safe!");
    }

    return 0;
}
```

The structure `features_seen` is declared to be of the `Features_t` struct type. All members of the `features_seen` structure are assigned `BIG`, which has the value `2`. The `features_seen` struct is passed as an argument into `wolf_test()`. At the beginning of `wolf_test()`, all four expressions are true and `features_big` is assigned a value of `1`. Therefore, since `features_big` has a non-zero value, the `if` statement in `wolf_test()` is evaluated to be true. A value of `1` is returned from the function and assigned to `big_result`. Therefore, `Oh no, it's a wolf!` is printed.

Since `scare_wolf()` returns a value of `G` that is assigned to `person_rescued`, the last `if` statement is true and `Granny and Little Red Riding Hood are safe!` is printed.

# The Princess and the Pea

Once upon a time, there was a prince who couldn't find a princess to marry. One stormy night, a girl arrived at the castle and said she was a princess. The king and queen let her into the castle to stay for the night in the guest room. The queen wanted to test if she was really a princess, so she put a pea on top of the bed's mattress and then stacked 20 mattresses on top of it. She then stacked 20 feather beds on top of that. "Sweet dreams!" said the queen.

```c
#include <stdio.h>

#define FALSE 0
#define TRUE 1
#define MATTRESS 2
#define FEATHER_BED 3
#define PEA 4

int main(void)
{
    int princess = FALSE;
    int sleep_quality;

    printf("Knock Knock\nWho's there?\nA princess\nA princess…who?\n");

    int bed_stack[41] = {0};

    for (int i = 0; i < 21; i++)
    {
        if (i == 0)
        {
            bed_stack[i] = PEA;
        }
        else
        {
            bed_stack[i] = MATTRESS;
        }
    }

    for (int i = 21; i < 41; i++)
    {
        bed_stack[i] = FEATHER_BED;
    }
```
**Continued…**

The `bed_stack` array's elements are all initialized to `0`. In the `for` loop, since `i` is initialized to `0` and the condition is `i < 21`, the loop executes 21 times. There is an `if…else` statement nested within the `for` loop. In the `for` loop's first iteration (when `i` has a value of `0`), `bed_stack[0]` is assigned a value of `4` (`PEA`). In all other iterations, `bed_stack[i]` is assigned a value of `2` (`MATTRESS`).

In the second `for` loop, `i` is initialized to `21` and since the condition is `i < 41`, the loop executes 20 times. For each iteration, `bed_stack[i]` is assigned a value of `3` (`FEATHER_BED`).

The queen decided that if the girl felt the pea under all the mattresses and feather beds, she must be a princess. After the girl woke up, the queen asked her how well she slept. The girl responded that she didn't sleep well at all because she felt a lump under the bed. The queen exclaimed, "You must be a princess!" and proceeded to put the pea into a glass case. The prince and (now) princess fell in love and got married. They lived happily ever after.

```c
printf("You are now going to sleep on a bed stacked with these items:\n");

for (int i = 0; i < 41; i++)
{
    if (bed_stack[i] == MATTRESS)
    {
        printf("Mattress (item #%d)\n", i);
    }
    else if (bed_stack[i] == FEATHER_BED)
    {
        printf("Feather bed (item #%d)\n", i);
    }
}

printf("\nSweet dreams!\n\n");

printf("How well did you sleep on a scale of 0-10?\n");

sleep_quality = 0;
printf("Definitely a %d\n", sleep_quality);

if (sleep_quality < 3)
{
    princess = TRUE;
}

if (princess)
{
    printf("Oh, you must be a princess!");
}

return 0;

} //end of main
```

This `for` loop executes `41` times. For each iteration, if the value of `bed_stack[i]` is equal to a value of `2` (`MATTRESS`), the nested `if` statement evaluates as true. This case occurs for `i = 1` through `i = 20`, since the first element of `bed_stack`, `bed_stack[0]`, was assigned a value of `4` (`PEA`). Elements `bed_stack[1]` through `bed_stack[20]` were each assigned a value of `2` (`MATTRESS`). For `i = 1`, `Mattress (item #1)` is printed.

For `i = 21` through `i = 40`, the `else if` statement is true because elements `bed_stack[21]` through `bed_stack[40]` were each assigned a value of `3` (`FEATHER_BED`). For `i = 21`, `Feather bed (item #21)` is printed.

The **less than operator** (<) is used to test if the value of `sleep_quality` is less than `3`. Since `sleep_quality` was assigned a value of `0`, the `if` statement is true, which assigns a value of `1` (`TRUE`) to `princess`. Therefore, the last `if` statement evaluates to true and `Oh, you must be a princess!` is printed.

# Cinderella

Once upon a time, a girl named Cinderella lived with her evil stepmother and two evil stepsisters. They made her do all their chores.

```c
#include <stdio.h>

#define NUM_ITEMS 4
#define STEPSISTER_ONE 1
#define STEPSISTER_TWO 2
#define CINDERELLA 3

typedef enum {PUMPKIN, MICE, RAT, OLD_DRESS} original_items_e;
typedef enum {CARRIAGE, HORSES, COACHMAN, NEW_GOWN} new_items_e;

void transform(original_items_e item);
void transform_back(new_items_e new_item);
char test_slipper(int person);
void slipper_test_result(char result);

void transform(original_items_e item)
{
    switch (item)
    {
        case PUMPKIN:
            printf("a carriage\n");
            break;
        case MICE:
            printf("horses\n");
            break;
        case RAT:
            printf("a coachman\n");
            break;
        case OLD_DRESS:
            printf("a new gown\n");
            break;
        default:
            break;
    }
}
```

**Continued...**

In *The Muffin Man* program, the `typedef` keyword was used to create a new name (alias) for a `struct` data type. In this program, `typedef` is used in `enum` definitions to create new `enum` data types called `original_items_e` and `new_items_e`. This allows you to declare `original_items_e` and `new_items_e` variables without using the `enum` keyword. The `transform()` function has a parameter called `item` that is of the `original_items_e` type. This means the function argument must be one of the `enum` constants in `original_items_e`. The `transform_back()` function has a parameter called `new_item` that is of the `new_items_e` type.

One day, a messenger arrived at the house with an invitation to meet Prince Charming at the royal ball. On the day of the ball, Cinderella was told she couldn't attend because she had too many chores to do. She was very upset, but suddenly out of nowhere her fairy godmother appeared and said she would help her get to the ball. The fairy godmother transformed a pumpkin into a carriage, mice into horses, a rat into a coachman, and Cinderella's old dress into a new gown. She also gave Cinderella two glass slippers. The fairy godmother told Cinderella the spell would wear off at midnight, at which time the transformed things would go back to their original states.

```c
void transform_back(new_items_e new_item)
{
    switch (new_item)
    {
        case CARRIAGE:
            printf("a pumpkin\n");
            break;
        case HORSES:
            printf("mice\n");
            break;
        case COACHMAN:
            printf("a rat\n");
            break;
        case NEW_GOWN:
            printf("an old dress\n");
            break;
        default:
            break;
    }
}

#define CHORES_NOT_DONE

int glass_slippers_num = 2;

int main(void)
{
    printf("Today, %s, is the ball!\n", __DATE__);

    #ifdef CHORES_NOT_DONE
        printf("I can't go to the ball since I have too many chores\n");
    #endif
```

**Continued...**

#ifdef is a **preprocessor directive** that stands for "if defined". It checks if a macro has been defined earlier in the code. This check happens before the code has been **compiled** (converted into machine language code the computer can understand). The CHORES_NOT_DONE macro is defined without any specific value, since for the purposes of #ifdef, it's not necessary for the tested macro to have a value—it only needs to be defined.

If the macro after #ifdef has been defined, the code between #ifdef and #endif is included in the program before it is compiled. Otherwise, if the macro has not been defined, this section of code is ignored. #ifdef is useful when you want code to be included in the program only in certain situations, such as when you're debugging (testing your code or finding the cause of "bugs" (errors)). In this program, since CHORES_NOT_DONE is defined, I can't go to the ball since I have too many chores is printed.

__DATE__ is a predefined macro in the C language. Before the program is compiled, the __DATE__ macro is replaced by a string that represents the current date.

ONE SIZE GLASS
DOES NOT FIT ALL SLIPPERS

Cinderella arrived at the ball at 8 o'clock. She danced with Prince Charming until she realized the clock was striking midnight and she promptly ran away. As she was running down the palace stairs, one of her glass slippers fell off and she didn't even notice.

```c
    printf("I'm your fairy godmother and I'll make your dreams come true.\n\n");
    printf("I am transforming the pumpkin into ");
    transform(PUMPKIN);
    printf("I am transforming the mice into ");
    transform(MICE);
    printf("I am transforming the rat into ");
    transform(RAT);
    printf("I am transforming your dress into ");
    transform(OLD_DRESS);

    printf("Oh, and I also got you %d glass slippers\n", glass_slippers_num);
    printf("The magic spell wears off at midnight. Have fun!\n\n");

    int hour = 8;

    while (hour <= 11)
    {
        printf("I'm dancing with Prince Charming!\n");
        printf("The clock just struck %d\n", hour);
        hour++; // This is the same as hour = hour + 1
    }

    printf("Oh no, it's midnight! Bye Prince Charming, I have to run!\n");

    // This is the same as glass_slippers_num = glass_slippers_num - 1
    glass_slippers_num--;

    if (glass_slippers_num % 2)
    {
        printf("Cinderella lost a glass slipper!\n");
    }
```

**Continued...**

The `transform()` function is called with arguments that are enum constants. In the first function call, `transform(PUMPKIN)`, the enum constant `PUMPKIN`, which holds a value of `0`, is passed as the argument. In `transform()`, the `switch` statement case corresponding to the value `0` is matched, which results in the printing of a carriage.

A `while` loop executes a block of code (within curly braces) if its condition is true, and repeats the code block's execution if its condition remains true after the code block executes. This process repeats until the condition evaluates to false, at which point the `while` loop ends and the program resumes executing after the loop. In this program, the `while` loop's condition uses the **less than or equal to operator** (<=) to test if the value of `hour` is less than or equal to `11`. The **increment operator** (++) increases the value of `hour` by `1` in each iteration of the `while` loop. The loop executes four times since `hour` is initialized to `8` and the loop repeats until `hour` is incremented to `12`.

The **decrement operator** (--) decreases the value of `glass_slippers_num` by `1`. The **modulus operator** (%) returns the remainder after the value on its left is divided by the value on its right. Since `glass_slippers_num` is now `1`, and the remainder of `1` divided by `2` is `1`, this non-zero remainder makes the `if` condition evaluate to true (any non-zero value evaluates to be true) and `Cinderella lost a glass slipper!` is printed.

She rode back home in the carriage, which soon turned back into a pumpkin. The horses turned back into mice, the coachman turned back into a rat, and her new gown turned back into her old dress. She walked the rest of the way home. Prince Charming found Cinderella's missing glass slipper on the stairs and was determined to find the girl it belonged to. When he went to Cinderella's house, her two stepsisters ran to the door and tried on the glass slipper. It did not fit either of them. Prince Charming noticed Cinderella cleaning upstairs and asked her to try on the glass slipper. It was a perfect fit! Cinderella and Prince Charming got married and lived happily ever after at the palace.

```c
    printf("\nThe magic spell is over. The following things are back:\n");
    transform_back(CARRIAGE);
    transform_back(HORSES);
    transform_back(COACHMAN);
    transform_back(NEW_GOWN);

    printf("\nI need to find the girl this glass slipper belongs to!\n");
    printf("The first stepsister is trying on the glass slipper\n");
    char result = test_slipper(STEPSISTER_ONE);
    slipper_test_result(result);
    printf("The second stepsister is trying on the glass slipper\n");
    result = test_slipper(STEPSISTER_TWO);
    slipper_test_result(result);
    printf("Prince Charming asked Cinderella to try on the glass slipper.\n");
    result = test_slipper(CINDERELLA);
    slipper_test_result(result);
    printf("\nCinderella and Prince Charming lived happily ever after.");
    return 0;
} //end of main

char test_slipper(int person)
{
    char result = (person == CINDERELLA) ? 'Y' : 'N';
    return result;
}

void slipper_test_result(char result)
{
    if (result == 'Y')
    {
        printf("The slipper is a perfect fit! She must be the girl I met at the ball!\n");
        glass_slippers_num++;
        printf("There are now %d glass slippers\n", glass_slippers_num);
    }
    else if (result == 'N')
    {
        printf("The slipper doesn't fit- she cannot be the girl I met at the ball\n");
    }
}
```

The **ternary operator**, used in the test_slipper() function, is a compact way of choosing one of two expressions to evaluate based on a condition. If the condition before the question mark is true, the ternary operator evaluates to the value of the first expression that is after the question mark. Otherwise, the ternary operator evaluates to the value of the expression that is after the colon (:). test_slipper(STEPSISTER_ONE) returns 'N' from the function. slipper_test_result() is then called with 'N' as the argument, which results in the printing of The slipper doesn't fit- she cannot be the girl I met at the ball. The next test_slipper() and slipper_test_result() function calls result in the same output. Lastly, since test_slipper(CINDERELLA) returns 'Y', the if statement in slipper_test_result() is executed.

# The Gingerbread Man

Once upon a time, an old woman and an old man lived in a cottage in the countryside. The old woman decided to make gingerbread cookies for dessert.

```c
#include <stdio.h>
#include <math.h>

#define INGREDIENTS_NUM 11

int main(void)
{
    enum ingredients_e {
            FLOUR, EGGS, BUTTER, BAKING_SODA, GROUND_GINGER,
            GROUND_CINNAMON, GROUND_CLOVES, GROUND_NUTMEG, SALT,
            GROUND_BLACK_PEPPER, DARK_BROWN_SUGAR
    };

    int ingredients[INGREDIENTS_NUM] = {
        FLOUR, EGGS, BUTTER, BAKING_SODA, GROUND_GINGER,
        GROUND_CINNAMON, GROUND_CLOVES, GROUND_NUTMEG, SALT,
        GROUND_BLACK_PEPPER, DARK_BROWN_SUGAR
    };

    float quantities[INGREDIENTS_NUM] = {3.0,2.0,0.75,0.75,0.75,1.0,0.5,0.5,0.5,0.25,0.5};

    // This recipe makes 20 gingerbread cookies. Enter an integer value.
    printf("How many gingerbread cookies do you want to make?\n");
    int cookie_num;
    scanf("%d", &cookie_num);
    int batches = ceil((float)cookie_num / 20); // round up to next batch number

    printf("\nA batch quantity of %d is needed to make %d cookies\n\n", batches, cookie_num);
    printf("The gingerbread cookie recipe calls for:\n");
```

**Continued...**

The elements of the ingredients array are initialized with enum constant values. The quantities array contains elements of the float data type, which are used to store **floating-point** numbers (numbers with a decimal point). Each of these float elements represents the quantity of the corresponding ingredient (at the same index) in the ingredients array.

The math.h header file, which is part of the C standard library, provides a variety of mathematical functions. Among these functions is ceil(), which returns the "ceiling" of a floating-point number by rounding it up to the nearest integer.

In C, the division of two integers results in another integer. If the actual result of the division is a fractional number, the fractional part is discarded, not rounded. To keep the fractional part, you can **typecast** the value (convert it into a different data type) by placing the desired data type in parentheses before the variable or value you want to convert. The scanf() function is used to read an integer value entered by the user and store it in cookie_num, which is then typecast to a float before it is divided by 20. The ceil() function is called on the result of this division. The value returned by ceil() indicates the total number of batches required to bake the desired number of cookies.

First, the old woman decided to make a unique gingerbread cookie in the shape of a man. She followed the gingerbread cookie recipe and mixed the ingredients.

```c
        for (int i = 0; i < INGREDIENTS_NUM; i++)
        {
            quantities[i] *= batches;

            switch (ingredients[i])
            {
                case FLOUR:
                    printf("%.2f cups of flour\n", quantities[i]);
                    break;
                case EGGS:
                    printf("%.2f eggs\n", quantities[i]);
                    break;
                case BUTTER:
                    printf("%.2f cups of butter\n", quantities[i]);
                    break;
                case BAKING_SODA:
                    printf("%.2f teaspoons of baking soda\n", quantities[i]);
                    break;
                case GROUND_GINGER:
                    printf("%.2f tablespoons of ground ginger\n", quantities[i]);
                    break;
                case GROUND_CINNAMON:
                    printf("%.2f tablespoons of ground cinnamon\n", quantities[i]);
                    break;
                case GROUND_CLOVES:
                    printf("%.2f teaspoons of ground cloves\n", quantities[i]);
                    break;
                case GROUND_NUTMEG:
                    printf("%.2f teaspoons of ground nutmeg\n", quantities[i]);
                    break;
                case SALT:
                    printf("%.2f teaspoons of salt\n", quantities[i]);
                    break;
                case GROUND_BLACK_PEPPER:
                    printf("%.2f teaspoons of ground black pepper\n", quantities[i]);
                    break;
                case DARK_BROWN_SUGAR:
                    printf("%.2f cups of dark brown sugar\n", quantities[i]);
                    break;
                default:
                    break;

            }

        }

    return 0;

} //end of main
```

In the first line of the for loop, the **multiplication compound-assignment operator** (*=) multiplies the current element of the quantities array by the value of batches. This operation is equivalent to quantities[i] = quantities[i] * batches and calculates the total quantity needed for the current ingredient based on the number of required batches. The %f in printf() is the format specifier used to print a float value. The .2 denotes that the float value should be printed to two decimal places.

The switch statement inside the for loop is used to check each element of the ingredients array against the constants declared in the ingredients_e enum. When a match is found, the corresponding quantity from the quantities array is printed, providing the measurement amount for that specific ingredient.

She baked the cookie at 350 °F for ten minutes. She opened the oven and much to her astonishment, the gingerbread man ran out! She chased after him. He shouted, "Run, run as fast as you can, you can't catch me, I'm The Gingerbread Man!" Next, the gingerbread man ran past the old man in the garden and shouted, "I've already run away from an old woman, and I can run away from you!" The old man ran and the gingerbread man shouted, "Run, run as fast as you can, you can't catch me, I'm The Gingerbread Man!" Next, the gingerbread man met a pig. He shouted, "I've already run away from an old woman, an old man, and I can run away from you!" The pig ran and the gingerbread man shouted, "Run, run as fast as you can, you can't catch me, I'm The Gingerbread Man!" Next, the gingerbread man met a cow. He shouted, "I've already run away from an old woman, an old man, a pig, and I can run away from you!" The cow ran and he shouted, "Run, run as fast as you can, you can't catch me, I'm The Gingerbread Man!" Next, the gingerbread man met a horse. He shouted, "I've already run away from an old woman, an old man, a pig, a cow, and I can run away from you!" The horse ran and he shouted, "Run, run as fast as you can, you can't catch me, I'm The Gingerbread Man!"

```c
#include <stdio.h>

enum {FALSE, TRUE};

const int num_chasers = 5;
int first_chaser = FALSE;

void bake_cookie(int temp, int minutes);
void gingerbread_man_speech(int chaser_num);

int main(void)
{
    printf("First, I will make a gingerbread cookie that looks like a person.\n");
    bake_cookie(350, 10);
    printf("Oh no, it's running away!\n");
    first_chaser = TRUE; //set the flag
    for (int i = 0; i < num_chasers; i++)
    {
        gingerbread_man_speech(i + 1);
    }

    printf("I'm a fox, hop on my back and I'll take you across the river\nNo!\n");
    gingerbread_man_speech(num_chasers + 1);

    return 0;
}
```

**Continued...**

In the function call bake_cookie(350, 10), the value 350 is passed to the temp parameter, and 10 is passed to the minutes parameter.

A **global variable**, such as num_chasers and first_chaser, is defined outside of any function and can be accessed by any function within the program. On the other hand, a **local variable** is defined within a function and can only be used within that function. A function's parameter is a local variable, and it can have a different name than the argument passed to it during the function call.

first_chaser is an example of a **flag variable**. The concept of a flag variable is tied to its value being in one of two states, commonly TRUE or FALSE. In this case, "setting the flag" means assigning it TRUE, and "clearing the flag" means assigning it FALSE.

The gingerbread man was eventually blocked by a river and met a fox that offered to take him across it. The gingerbread man hopped on his back, but once the fox asked him to hop on his nose, the gingerbread man became nervous and was able to hop onto the other side of the river instead. The gingerbread man escaped and ran away.

```c
void bake_cookie(int temp, int minutes)
{
    printf("I'm baking the cookie at %d deg F for %d minutes\n", temp, minutes);
    while (minutes > 0)
    {
        minutes--;
        printf("Timer: %d\n", minutes);
    }
    printf("It's ready!\n");
}

void gingerbread_man_speech(int chaser_num)
{
    if (first_chaser)
    {
        first_chaser = FALSE; //clear the flag
    }
    else
    {
        printf("I've already run away from:\n");
        for (int i = 0; i <= chaser_num; i++)
        {
            if (i == chaser_num)
            {
                printf("and I can run away from you, ");
            }

            switch (i)
            {
                case 1:
                    printf("old woman\n");
                    break;
                case 2:
                    printf("old man\n");
                    break;
                case 3:
                    printf("pig\n");
                    break;
                case 4:
                    printf("horse\n");
                    break;
                case 5:
                    printf("cow\n");
                    break;
                case 6:
                    printf("fox\n");
                    break;
                default:
                    break;
            }
        }
    }

    printf("Run, run, as fast as you can, you can't catch me, I'm the Gingerbread Man!\n\n");
}
```

# Run the Programs!

Now you can share the nursery rhymes and fairy tales with YOUR computer! You can run the programs on your computer using a **C compiler**, which converts your **source code** (the code you wrote) into **machine code** that the computer can execute. There are many free C compilers available online. If you search for "free online C compiler", you'll find compilers that run online without requiring a download. This is the link to a good online C compiler called **Online GDB**:

https://www.onlinegdb.com/online_c_compiler

Type the code in the editor and click the green **Run** button at the top. You'll see the output of the `printf()` functions in the console at the bottom.

## Common Errors

Code editors highlight different types of code with different colors, which is called **syntax highlighting**. For example, comments are all highlighted with the same color. This makes the code easier to read.

If you get an error message after running the code, fix the code and run it again! There are many common **syntax errors**. **Make sure to:**

- Correctly use the assignment operator ( = ) and equality operator ( == ).
- End every statement with a semicolon ( ; )
- Insert the correct number of quotation marks and parentheses, and place them correctly. You'll also get an error if you copy and paste quotes (such as from a word processor) written in unicode format (`"Hi!"`) rather than ASCII format (`"Hi!"`). When you type quotation marks directly into the code editor, it will be in ASCII format.
- Use open and closing curly braces around code blocks, including function bodies, loops (such as `for` and `while`), and conditional statements (such as `if` and `else`). Although a code block containing only one statement doesn't require curly braces, it's good practice to include braces in case more lines are added in the future.

You are now a C programmer!

## Change the Stories

Change the values of variables and see how the output changes. What if Jack didn't fall down the hill?

## Why C Programming?

Dennis Ritchie developed the C programming language at Bell Laboratories in the early 1970s. Many features of C programming were adopted by popular high-level languages like C++, Java, and Python. A high-level language is designed to be easily understood by humans, using words and phrases similar to everyday language. In contrast, a low-level language is closer to machine code, which gives programmers precise control over the computer's inner hardware operations. The C language uniquely combines both, as it offers high-level logical constructs like `if...else` statements and loops, while also allowing for low-level control, notably through pointers that access the computer's memory. The C language is widely used in many areas including computer games, graphics, desktop software, operating systems, databases, and embedded systems. By learning C, you are building a strong foundation in the world of computer programming.

## You Don't Need a Magic Wand

C is the most popular language in embedded systems! An embedded system is a hardware and software system designed to perform one or more specific tasks within a larger system. A **microcontroller** is a common type of embedded system that is in devices and appliances all around you, like your phone, printer, microwave, washing machine, and remote control—just to name a few. Now you can make things move by programming them!

A microcontroller has all the components of a computer contained in a single chip (integrated circuit or IC). Just like your computer reads input from the keyboard and outputs text to the screen, a microcontroller reads **inputs** (such as from a sensor or button) and controls **outputs** (such as turning on an LED or motor). This allows the embedded system to sense and interact with the outside world.

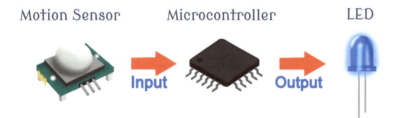

You can apply the syntax and constructs you learned in this book to programming microcontrollers, so you can create your own devices. The Arduino® is a popular microcontroller development platform. The Arduino language is a set of C/C++ functions that you call from your code. For more information about the Arduino platform, please visit: https://www.arduino.cc

Arduino® is a trademark of Arduino SA

# More programming books by Shari Eskenas

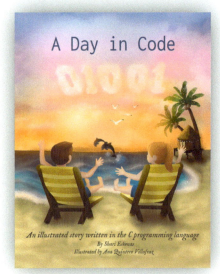

**A Day in Code**
An illustrated story written in
the C programming language
ISBN: 978-1-73590-791-8 (paperback)
978-1-73590-790-1 (hardcover)

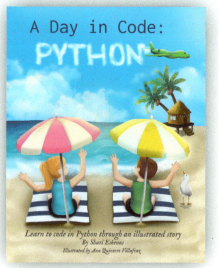

**A Day in Code- Python**
Learn to code in Python
through an illustrated story
ISBN: 978-1-73590-794-9 (paperback)
978-1-73590-793-2 (hardcover)

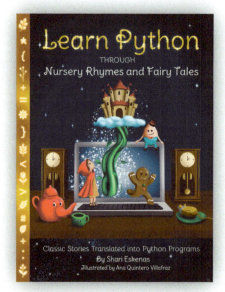

**Learn Python through Nursery Rhymes and Fairy Tales**
Classic Stories Translated into Python Programs
ISBN: 978-1-73590-798-7 (paperback)
978-173590-796-3 (hardcover)

You're Invited

Join the celebration at
www.sundaelectronics.com/Cfairytales

www.ingramcontent.com/pod-product-compliance
Lightning Source LLC
LaVergne TN
LVHW071943070326
832904LV00036B/307